Worshipful Master's Guidebook

OR

THE "BOOK OF JOE"

Bro.

JAMES F. HATCHER III, P.M.

ISBN-13: 978-1493751792
ISBN-10: 1493751794

Available from Amazon.com, CreateSpace.com, and other retail outlets

www.CreateSpace.com/4523383

Printed by CreateSpace, Charleston SC
An Amazon.com Company

DEDICATION

This book is dedicated to all Past Masters, past, present and future, of our beloved Fraternity, which we call Freemasonry, but especially to my friend and big Brother, Joe Malcolm Mencer, who roped me into becoming a line officer in my Masonic Lodge, which later led to my appointment and eventual election as Worshipful Master of my Lodge. It was an eighteen month period of my life in which the words in this book proved to be of great benefit during my time of service in the Oriental Chair.

Without this advice, I would have surely been lost in the East.

With this advice, hopefully you will not be either.

PRESENTED TO

_____

Lodge and Number

_____

By

_____

Date of Presentation

CONTENTS

ACKNOWLEDGMENTS

Special kudos go out to the Past Masters of Rockford Masonic Lodge No. 469, Free and Accepted Masons of Tennessee, for their unwavering support, continual guidance and wise advice, but especially those who helped me on my personal journey through the Chairs:

Brother PMs:

Joe Mencer, Jason Deck, Larry Price, Carl Reneau, David Williamson, David Williams, Mike Weems, Frank Proctor, Brian Proctor, Garry Wackerhagen, Doug Cable, Jason Ford, Donnie Dykes, Bobby Pollard, Jerry White, Curly Wainwright, Richard Hines, Jerry Brackett, Dennis Effler, Eddie Everhart, Bill Neubert, Daniel Mata, and Tom Boduch PGM.

1 INTRODUCTION

The inspiration for writing this book came one November night, when I received a phone call from our Senior Warden, Joe Mencer, asking me to consider taking the appointed position of Junior Deacon in our Masonic Lodge for the upcoming year. He advised that it was a five-year commitment, not one but five. He stated that it would be an "interesting journey" and that I could "write that down." I literally scribbled "interesting journey" on my notepad from work while we talked, and I advised that I would probably be interested. Bro. Joe told me to take some time and think about it, talk it over with my wife, and then call him back and let him know. I did, and it was indeed a very, interesting journey.

Along the way, I took the time over the next several years to jot down many Joe-isms, as Joe was continually saying, "You'll need to know this when you get in the East." He, along with many others, would often give little tidbits of wisdom in conversation, which I would write down for future reference. Sometimes, these would be comical and sometimes these would be serious, but they were all seemingly relevant to the general success of the Lodge and/or Masonry at the time, so I wrote them down. Over time, my collection of Masonic wisdom became informally known within the walls of our Lodge, as the Book of Joe.

Somewhere along the way, I was elected by my Brothers as the Senior Warden of our Lodge. At our annual Past Masters' Meeting the previous year, I was asked by the Past Masters of our Lodge, that "if some unfortunate event should occur next year with the Worshipful Master" (i.e., loss of life, serious injury or illness, change of employment, incapacitation, etc.), if I felt that I would be able to assume the duties in the East in his stead. Of course, I naturally said YES. After all, the State Masonic Code specifically stated that the Worshipful Master could not resign during his year, and incapacitation in any form is rare under most usual conditions.

On a sunny Saturday Morning in June, I left with two other Brothers to go to an out-of-town Masonic meeting on the planning of events for our Grand Lodge's Bicentennial the following year. At High Noon I was the Senior Warden of our Lodge. At 3:32 PM, the Grand Master appointed me Worshipful

Master pro Tempore of our Lodge by phone. He had granted a medical leave of absence to our Worshipful Master, and I was to finish the remainder of his term. No warning, no advanced notice, just a phone call of immediate appointment.

This resulted in my appointment and eventual election as Worshipful Master...a term of eighteen months in all. No preparation time, no time to question or ponder, and no anticipation. It was real and it was in effect immediately.

It was at this time, in a state of controlled panic, that I reached for the notebook of Past Master advice that I had been writing down for years to see where the answers were. Many, many times over the next year and a half, I revisited this notebook. Sometimes I read, and sometimes I wrote. This wisdom guided me through that period of my life that one calls, "My year as Master," and compelled me to put these writings in print.

This book has been designed for use by Masonic Lodges, to be continually updated each year and passed from one Master to the next with continual updates of bits of wisdom by succeeding Masters. It is, in some ways, the Masonic Book of Secrets for the Worshipful Master. Unlike that mysterious fabled book passed down from U.S. President to U.S. President, this one is real.

If you are a current Past Master, purchase a copy for your Lodge, write in your advice, have the other Past Masters write in theirs and present it to your Worshipful Master to be handed down through the years in your Lodge.

If you are the current Worshipful Master of your Lodge, purchase a copy of this book and fill in your tidbits of wisdom for your successor and those to follow him.

Bro. James Frank "Chip" Hatcher III
Past Master
Rockford No. 469 F&AM
Rockford, Tennessee

...and as the Sun rules the day,
and the Moon governs the night,
so should the Worshipful Master
rule and govern the Lodge
with equal regularity...

but...
with a little common sense
and basic training.

2 ADVICE FROM THOSE BEFORE ME

1. Communicate – communicate – communicate!

2. Communicate constantly with your officers. At least every other day with your Wardens and at least weekly with your appointed officers.

3. If you make everybody happy, you didn't do your job.

4. Pick officers that want to work and aren't afraid to get their hands dirty.

5. If you make everyone mad, no one will come back. It is a voluntary organization. They don't work for you, they pay to have you ask them to help you.

6. They don't have to support you; they can stay at home and watch TV on Stated Meeting nights and Lodge Events.

7. Many of our Lodge members are older "drug addicts"—legally, through prescribed medicine from legitimate doctors—but they often exhibit the same behaviors and symptoms in their thinking and actions. Medicine makes men do, think and say strange things. It's not personal. Be aware of this!

8. You can't make everyone happy, so don't try.

9. Sometimes, you're up there in the East and you know every member is making the absolutely wrong decision on a matter. As Worshipful Master, you have to let them do it, even if you know it is absolutely the wrong decision. There is nothing you can do about it. It is their right to do so.

10. Never get caught with your pants down in the East. You should know everything that is going on in the Lodge, so you won't be surprised when it is brought up on the Lodge floor.

11. You cannot introduce a motion on the floor. If you have something you want addressed, have one of your officers introduce it.

12. Make sure you have an agenda before you open the meeting...and stick to it.

13. Never allow a vote on a critical issue on the night the issue is brought up. Lay it over until next month, appoint a committee if you need to, but give the issue some time

for discussion, instead of allowing it to be ramrodded through in one night.

14. If it involves spending money, lay it over until next month if at all possible, unless the Treasurer says it is an emergency and its okay or a have-to-right-now thing.

15. There will be many opinions on every issue. Listen to them all and make your decision for the "good of the Lodge" not for the good of a brother...and NEVER for the good of yourself.

16. Make sure your Secretary and Treasurer can work together...seamlessly together.

17. There are some brothers who bitch about everything. Don't let them drag you down. Thank them for their concern and move on. You can't make them happy, anyway, no matter what you do. Don't get tied up in their drama.

18. NEVER serve as an officer in an Appendant or Concordant Body that meets in your Lodge during your year as Master.

19. Maintain good relationships with the Eastern Star, but ALWAYS remember it is a MASONIC LODGE, not an OES CHAPTER HOUSE.

20. Never print tickets to an event on a letter. If you do, then they become coupons and will be given all the attention and concern and interest that coupons are given. When

you do this, your event will be a flop. Tickets are tickets and should be printed and cut like tickets. When you "coupon" them, then people treat them like coupons and, unless they clip and use coupons, the letter will end up in the trash and you will have wasted a lot of lodge money.

21. Your year as Master is solely dependent upon your officer corps. If they do good, you will be remembered as a good Master; if they do bad, you will be known as a bad master.

22. Don't worry about what people think or say about your decisions. It is easy to criticize another. Do what you think is right and is the right course and what is best for the lodge.

23. Always remember that in 100 years, the masons of our Lodge will look at your picture and talk about the way things were then, unless you screw it up and loose the lodge...then...they will never exist.

24. Past Masters are a very valuable resource for the Master, but remember ALWAYS, they are PAST Masters. What happened in their year was in their year. You will be dealing with your own set of unique circumstances in your own specific time. What they did in their year may or may not work in yours. Theirs is advice, not dictation. Once you are a Past Master, then again, you are just a regular Master Mason on the sidelines.

25. After your year in the East, be busy in January and February and March...very busy. LAY DOWN THE GAVEL AND WALK AWAY. The Immediate Past Master's

job is to advise when asked, not continue to preside through the new Master.

26. Pick a Chaplain that is an old and wise Past Master.

27. Pick a Tyler that knows EVERYONE.

28. What happens in our Lodge, stays in our Lodge. Do not discuss internal business with members of other Lodges. It is none of their business. If they ask, don't play into that. Inform them that the issue is internal and not up for discussion. Invite them to become a plural member, and you can talk about it all they want.

29. DO NOT allow members of other lodges drag their Lodge's dirty laundry into yours.

30. If they will not stop nosing into our Lodge business or won't stop trying to drag our Lodge into theirs, ask them to leave the premises.

31. GOSSIP HAS NO ROLE IN FREEMASONRY.

32. Don't plan your year in the East out. Have a tentative plan for presentation to the Brethren. If the Lodge thinks it is a good idea and wants to do it, it will be great. If not, then it won't. The calendar has to be thought out, planned and executed by the members. If they have no say in what the Lodge is doing, then there is no reason for them to pay dues and attend. No voice in the happenings of the Lodge means no money in the bank and no one in attendance at the event. If you dictate all the events, then

you are a dictator, passive or active, you are a dictator. It is your job to devise a plan, and it is the lodge's job to approve, amend or disapprove of it. Work your plan and ideas on the floor of the Lodge through your officers and at Officer Meetings.

33. Officer Meetings are where you finalize the proposals to the Lodge. Before a proposal is made on the floor of the Lodge, make sure you have a really good feeling that it will pass or be seriously considered. Don't just throw it out there for discussion. Don't run on the battlefield looking for options and ammunition for your empty gun. Be prepared before you make the assault.

34. DON'T SERVE HOTDOGS unless you have to. People come for a good meal and will make donations into the kitchen bucket if you serve good food. If the food is bad, the donation bucket will be empty, and you will be buying the food for the next meal.

35. Greet everyone who comes into the Lodge and thank them for coming. Make it a priority to know a little something about what they have been doing, how their wife or kids are, how something in their life is going, etc.

36. DO NOT FORGET THE WIDOWS. Do something for them a couple of times a year. When you do it, make sure it is done right and very nicely done. Never forget YOUR wife will be a Masonic Widow one day (law of averages).

37. Make sure the Lodge is cleaned up ON THE SAME DAY the event is held. Do not let the mess lie. Other people

use the Lodge. Problems are bugs, visitors who may stop by and look in the door, brothers who bring a prospect by to see the Lodge.

38. Make sure you have petitions on hand for visitors. Don't look like a damned goober when a man asks for a petition, and "you can't find one, but will get back with him." This is bad...very bad business, and it sends a very bad "we don't want you" signal to the prospective member.

39. Your brothers will break your heart. They don't mean to, but, eventually, they will break your heart at some point, either by their death or their actions. You still need to love them. It will eventually all work out. We are, after all, brothers...not friends or acquaintances.

40. Pep yourself up before the stated meeting, especially if you feel it is going to be a heated one. Never go into battle without your armor.

41. Know the code book long before you are Master.

42. You serve at the will of the Grand Master and are charged to protect and defend the charter of the Lodge. If you fail in this duty, nothing else matters.

43. When you appoint a chairman over some committee and event, ensure that he knows that it is HIS deal to work, not yours. This includes the primary responsibility for making sure communication occurs, project or event is planned and that it is effectively executed. If the

chairman you appoint can't get the job done, it is not your job to complete the task...appoint someone else to make sure that it gets done.

44. Make sure your officers know their duties.

45. The Senior Warden is in charge of masons while the Lodge is at Labor: this includes, work projects, fundraisers, degree work, meetings, charity events, ANYTHING done in the public eye. He is the primary leader in this arena.

46. The Junior Warden is in charge of masons while at REFRESHMENT. This includes dinner events, luncheons, social events, the kitchen, festive boards, menus, etc.

47. The Deacons are in charge of welcoming everyone who visits our Lodge, members and non-members alike. They also assist the Senior Warden and Worshipful Master, as needed or required. They also set up the Lodge Room before meetings and put everything in its place afterwards.

48. The Stewards assist the Junior Warden in his duties. They are also assist in cooking and preparing to eat, lodge housekeeping and maintenance.

49. The Stewards are to ensure the dining hall is mopped and cleaned before every meeting and event held in our Lodge, as well as the bathrooms and exterior checked for cleanliness and orderliness. No one wants to eat in a greasy spoon.

50. I have been in some Lodges, where the same spider webs have been in the same windows for years. Memorabilia are those things the Lodge keeps and preserves over the ages. Spider webs are not part of that.

51. The Junior Warden is to ensure the kitchen is left clean and orderly after every event. Other people use our Lodge during the month, and should have the expectation of not cleaning up our messes before their events.

52. We have a day-use kitchen. If there are leftovers, they either go home with someone or go in the trash can outside. No one is going to make a midnight snack on Wednesday night out of our refrigerator....ever. We don't live here, even though it may seem like it sometimes.

53. If we leave food out on the counter, we are feeding and breeding rats, flies and roaches.

54. Yesterday, we had 1 fly in here, and you left the doors propped open all day. Today we have 13.

55. Make sure the candidate knows about the degree fee BEFORE you ask him the questions.

56. Don't allow yourself to become overburdened...get some help...it is called delegation. If you can't delegate, you're screwed from the git-go.

57. Count the ballot...twice...before you destroy it.

58. Don't allow the membership to talk, and especially argue, across the Lodge. Maintain an orderly discussion.

59. Don't be afraid to rap a brother down to maintain peace and harmony in the Lodge. It is your duty to do so.

60. Don't let a brother ramble on in Lodge about any and everything.

61. So long as he is on point within the current discussion, a brother may vice his concern or speak his mind. If he strays from the topic at hand, do not allow him to use the Lodge floor a forum to reinforce his own personal agenda.

62. Turn your cell phone ringer off or on vibrate before the meeting.

63. Respect and allow the opinions of each man in the Lodge, so long as they are constructive and not crafted for ill means.

64. On change, the definition of peace and harmony for a long time in a pond is called stagnant water.

65. If you don't visit other Lodges, don't expect to have very many visitors to yours.

66. All we do is for vanity, thus sayeth the preacher.

67. Maintain a 5-year plan, Stewards excluded. It is every Master's job to appoint his replacement (hopefully) to the bottom of the line. The Steward positions give a man an

opportunity to see if he likes serving as an officer in the line, but they are not (in most Lodges) part of the 5-year plan of succession.

68. Plan your events a minimum of 3 months out. This gives enough time for everyone to discuss the pros and cons, formulate a solid proposal and introduce it to the Lodge, so no one can say, "They ramrodded that one through."

69. Do not plan events in October/November/December to be held in the new term in January/February/March... "it ain't your year anymore"...with the exception of very large events, which may "need 8-12 months to prepare for. Again, this should be discussed with the Senior Warden, if it appears there is a good chance he will be the next Master AND it will occur in his year. One possibility would be to appoint a planning committee to brainstorm the idea or event, with the Senior Warden as Chairman. Let the Senior Warden pick his committee members.

70. Appoint Committee Chairmen, then let them pick their Committee Members. Have this all worked out before the Stated Meeting, if at all possible.

71. Don't plan anything big in January and February. You need to settle in to the job before charging forth into glory.

72. Sometimes, there is just this feeling of impending doom looming about.

73. Most highly effective leaders were not the most popular ones.

74. Don't make the Lodge "what it used to be" back then; make it what it should be right now.

75. Don't send any correspondence out with bad or incorrect grammar. Proof read everything and ensure it is correct. Remember your stairwell lecture in the Fellow Craft.

76. Get your lecture and proficiency cards before you become Master.

77. Masonry is like a redneck marriage – it's the little stuff that just tears it apart.

78. When you start a new program, and it's working...let it do what you started it to do and baby it till it's working the way you want it to.

79. You don't throw away your life preserver because you see land on the horizon!

80. THERE ARE NO OLD PAST MASTERS AND OLDER MEMBERS WHO ARE GOING TO COME IN AND SHUT YOU AND YOUR OFFICER TEAM DOWN FOR YOUR NEW, INNOVATIVE IDEAS BECAUSE THEY DO NOT AGREE WITH YOU. This is an old myth created by contrary men with control issues who can't grasp that they are no longer in charge and cannot accept the fact that it will, and cannot, be like it was eons ago when they were responsible for running the Lodge. Don't worry,

they will get over it in due time, return to the Lodge...or they won't.

81. REMEMBER, when you appoint your committees for the year, keep in mind that the Lodge elected YOU and your officers to run the operation of the Lodge for the next year, NOT the corps of Past Masters to dictate to you what you should do to make them happy.

82. Appoint your Officers as the heads of the committees, and place a Past Master on the committee to help guide him.

83. If you fill your Committee Chairmen seats with Past Masters instead of your officers, do not expect much results. Past Masters are a wealth of advice, but do little in most cases, when it comes to providing the necessary drive to charge forth into the year with fervor and zeal to accomplish their mission. They had their day in charge, and most don't want to chair anything. Place that in the hands of the new guys with new ideas.

84. Standing Committees are those committees you are required to appoint as required by the Grand Lodge directives or the Lodge By-Laws (e.g., Audit, Budget, Finance, Charity, Membership, Visiting, etc.). Appoint them as required.

85. Special Committees are those committees that serve a specific function, which are not required, but needed, that you must appoint. (e.g., Past Masters' Night, Widows' Christmas Baskets, Lodge building or service

project, Parade Float, etc.). Appoint them as needed. The less you have, the easier it will be.

86. It is NOT spelled M-A-S-O-N-A-R-Y. That is not a word in the English Language. Don't embarrass yourself in front of your more informed Brethren by writing or speaking it. It is MASONRY (May-son-ree). It amazes me how many plaques, certificates and news articles use this strange spelling of the word.

87. If you have more than two things on you To-Do List, you have too many. As you finish one, you may add another, but never more than two at a time.

88. Have a reception at your installation, big or small, but have a reception. Have it AFTER the Officer installation, never before. If you have it before, then 15 minutes after your Installation is over, everyone will be gone. You can sit there in your Lodge by yourself and be happy.

89. The Office of Worshipful Master is where you truly learn Fortitude, Prudence, Temperance and Justice, but most of all, it is the greatest exercise in Patience that any man can endure, outside of war and raising children.

90. Grand Lodge Officers are either: (1) Visitors to your Lodge, or (2) Members of your Lodge. They do not preside, control, govern or command your lodge, so unless the Grand Master himself comes into your Lodge and takes your gavel to preside (then, it's his meeting), you are in charge of maintaining the peace and harmony and charter of your Lodge that you have opened.

91. Serving in the East is a most anticipated event in one's life before service, the most challenging during service, and the most relieving after service.

92. In most normal situations, and if you do it right, you should only be asked to sit in the Oriental Chair one time; therefore, you only get to do this once, so do it right the first time. If you get to do it again, the second time does not count and certainly will not be as fruitful, successful, nor as special as the first time around.

93. When your year as Worshipful Master in the East is over, then it is over. Hand over the gavel to your successor, sit down, and shut up. It's not about you anymore, it's about the next guy. You're done, brother.

94. Don't be the proverbial pain in the butt for those who follow you.

3 MY ADVICE TO YOU

4 ADVICE FROM THE GUY AFTER ME

_____

_____

_____

_____

_____

_____

_____

_____

_____

_____

_____

_____

5 ADVICE FROM THE GUY AFTER HIM

_____

_____

_____

_____

_____

_____

_____

_____

_____

6 ADVICE FROM THE GUYS AFTER US

_____

_____

_____

_____

_____

_____

_____

_____

_____

_____

_____

_____

_____

_____

_____

_____

_____

_____

_____

_____

_____

_____

_____

_____

_____

_____

_____

_____

_____

_____

_____

_____

_____

_____

_____

_____

_____

_____

_____

_____

_____

_____

_____

_____

_____

_____

_____

_____

_____

_____

_____

_____

_____

_____

_____

_____

_____

_____

_____

_____

_____

_____

_____

_____

_____

_____

_____

_____

_____

_____

_____

_____

_____

_____

_____

_____

_____

_____

_____

_____

_____

_____

_____

_____

_____

_____

_____

_____

_____

_____

_____

_____

_____

_____

_____

_____

_____

_____

_____

_____

_____

_____

_____

_____

_____

_____

_____

_____

_____

_____

_____

_____

_____

_____

_____

_____

_____

_____

_____

_____

_____

_____

_____

_____

_____

_____

_____

_____

_____

_____

_____

_____

_____

_____

_____

_____

_____

_____

_____

_____

_____

_____

_____

_____

_____

_____

_____

_____

_____

_____

_____

_____

_____

_____

_____

_____

_____

_____

_____

_____

_____

_____

_____

_____

_____

_____

_____

_____

_____

_____

_____

_____

ABOUT THE AUTHOR

Bro. James Frank Hatcher III, better known as "Chip," is a Master Mason and Past Worshipful Master of Rockford Masonic Lodge No. 469, Free and Accepted Masons of Tennessee, in Rockford, Tennessee ~ a small, quiet hamlet in the foothills of the Great Smoky Mountains in Eastern Tennessee. He lives with his wife, three children, three dogs, six cats, two hermit crabs, and nearby to many, many wonderful friends, whom he later found to be his Brothers in many, many different situations.

He is also the Author of the:

Lodge Officer's Handbook
https://www.createspace.com/4527286

and

King Solomon's Passport
https://www.createspace.com/4531237

SO·MOTE·IT·BE